Whispers of my Notes App

POETRY BOOK

White Hunter

Whispers Of My Notes App

For the little poet, who thought her poems were a waste and dumped them into The Notes app.

This is for you and your little dream of becoming an Author:)

Index

Holding Hands With Death

I asked death
Walking by my side
Silently holding my hand
From the day I first cried,

"How will it feel
when you come to me?"
"Will it be painful
Or will I feel free?"
Not saying a word
She starred into my eye
So I asked again
"Will I be happy or will it be a hurtful goodbye?"

Waited for the words that never came
But I pictured her smile
As if telling me
We still have to walk a mile,

While entering another street of fate
My heart questions again
"If I want to stay a little more,
Will you wait?"

The smile I pictured
Got lost somewhere
Because we both knew
The answer lying unspoken in the air,

Without another word
I tightened my grip around her hand
And started leaving footprints
On life's soft sand.

_WH

Preplanned Funeral

Funerals are sad I know
But be happy on mine
So I can sleep peacefully
Six feet under the sign,

A fine-cut stone piece sign
Above my grave
That says a beautiful name
My mother gave,

A black wooden coffin with a pillow would be fine
With a white wollen blanket
My grandma once design,

Please don't mourn or cry
Over my polished coffin
If you miss me then
Why don't you come and join in?

Don't decorate my funeral with
Old traditional white flowers
Use some daisies or orchids
That represents the memories of ours,

There's no point in coming to my grave
Leaving your job or home all behind
While you don't even come to say
Hello, when I still have some time,

Please don't recite sad eulogies or
Long speeches that are boring
I don't want people at my funeral
Sleeping or snoring,

Sing some songs or
Play some karaoke instead
Dance and enjoy
Songs of Coldplay and weeknd,

Make my funeral unforgettable
Something beautifully remarkable,

Funerals are sad I know
But on mine, be happy and smiling
So that I can die peacefully
Without leaving anyone behind, sad and crying.

_WH

Glimpse Of My Broken Heart

It's not just a poem
But a glimpse of my broken heart
Waiting for someone
To heal my wounds,

These are not just some lines
Written by a pen
But the thoughts
That caused this overwhelming pain,

Words
That left deep scars
That can't be fixed
Like a broken glass,

Wish someone hears
The silent screams of my soul
But in this never-ending universe
I am still alone,

Fighting
The huge rough sorrowful waves
Don't know how long
My paper boat will sail,

Lost the hope
Of someone holding my hand
Now it's just me
Only me in my dream fairyland,

It’s not just a poem
But a glimpse of my broken heart
That has now stopped waiting for that someone
And given my fallen world a fresh start.

_WH

Accidental Writer

I wanted to be everything in my life
But not a writer
I wanted to scream, shout, and fight for everything
But my timid self couldn't be a fighter,

Now it feels like
Writing has become an intricate part of my life
The only thing
That's keeping me alive,

I write love, pain, joy, fear,
Anxiety, depression,
I write my every tear,
I've come to a point
from where there is no going back,
Or maybe it was me
Who covered all my tracks

I didn't want to go back to normal living,
This is what I want
A tragic yet beautiful feeling,
Craved in my mind soul and heart,
As I weaved the words in my written art,

I write for him I write for her,
I write for every soul screaming
with pain, none could hear,

I still don't want to be a writer
But I guess it's too late
The childhood me with my dreams buried in her
Looks at me as if telling me it was all written in my fate.

_WH

The Reality I Wanna Run Away

I'm in my psych class
Not paying attention
Only looking at my notes
Seeing my own reflection,

The white paper
Pretending to be a mirror
Showing me
My worst figure,

The site was so horrible
That my anxiety started to take over,

My lungs were breathless
Grasping for air
With a blurred sight
My heart started beating at the speed of light
Then,

Then everything stopped
Every voice
Every scream
Every word in the air
Stopped,

Teacher called me
But I didn't hear
Maybe because
I just wanted to disappear,

At last, she shouted
Tired of trying
Three words formed in my throat
That says, “I am fine.”

_WH

Wandering Freak

I don't like curtailing my freedom
I like to be free
Like a bird swaying its wings
In the blue sky
Or random dreams
Lingering in my Brown eyes,

Call it insane
but I don't feel like staying in the same place
I love to scatter around
Like dandelions searching for solace,

I'm a wandering freak
I know
I embrace my world-changing fast
And sometimes slow,

I walk, I run around the roads of earth
But sometimes through the streets of my own mind,
Searching somewhere
Where the stars of my fate aligned,

I'm not a history nerd
But I like cities where life is older than tree
Somewhere near the mountains
Or sometimes closer to the sea,

Lying here on the green Ocean
Under the blanket weaved with star
Sometimes I wonder
How someone staying in the same room
Could go so far?

_WH

A Late Night Over Thinker Heart

It's me against my own self
Fighting my own battles
The pieces of my heart
Still rattles,

Even when everything outside
Is quiet
Something is going on inside me
Like a neverending riot,

One part of me says
I can do a lot with my life
But the other says
It's not so good to be alive,

Maybe I look like the world's happiest person
Outside
But there is something hidden
Always inside,

Sick of this pointless
Societal morality
Music has always been
An escape from reality,

The words of people
Penetrating deep inside my heart
Still my tears
Forms the most beautiful art,

Sometimes it feels like I'm an experiment
Continuously put through tests
Where I'm doing worse
Then rests,

I just want to go
Far far away from this place
Where I don't need to regret
My mistake,

Lost somewhere
In the space
Where I don't feel
Like a disgrace
Somewhere
Where I am embraced,

It's me against my own self
Fighting my own battles
The pieces of my heart
Still rattles.

_WH

Losing The Touch In Poetry

Things will never be the same
As it was before
Losing the touch in poetry
Because the little heart
Can't take it anymore,

Burning with rage
Warmth of grief
Even in the calmest darkness,
It couldn't find relief,

Now I'm sitting in a war
Hoping to find serenity,
Picking up the words
Weaving into a tapestry,

Waiting for them to lay me
Next to a nameless grave of a Young English poet
While Hearing the waters
Whispering my poems in the quiet

_WH

Twilight

Life went on but I got left
Somewhere in the moments of that night,
The time when leaving me behind
Suddenly felt right,

The time
Which was neither day nor night,
But the moments somewhere between
The twilight,

When I was pretty, beautiful,
And young
The same time when I left everything
Like a song, unsung,

Strangely for the first time in my life,
Everything felt quite
Like I have finally won
The long-lost fight,

From being afraid of the world,
hiding myself within,
I finally freed from the cage
Of miles-long skin,

From drowning in air
To drowning in actual water,
I survived my life
But still wonder why it was shorter.

_WH

Secrets Nature Beholds

Sitting on the grass
Under the blue ocean
Trying to understand me
And the world's tragic notion

I was thinking, writing
And even scribbling a little,
Then A voice nested in my ears,
Like a cry that made me unsettle,

Following the noise
I came in front of an old oak tree
There was this little birdie
Pleading to be free,

Cautiously with care
And lots of love
I freed her from the net
She flew above,

I Came back to my spot
Started thinking like a nerdy Thinker,
There she came again
Sat softly on my finger,

Fearlessly sitting, she tilted
Gazed at me with her blue eyes

As if telling me the truths
Hidden in the skies,

I stared into her eyes
We started gossiping like friends,
I told her about my life while she whispered
The first truth lies where the sky ends,

In her eyes, I saw a glimpse
Of the changing human race,
The one that cherished love, poems, and pain
Now started hiding behind a blank face,

The wind secretly passed by us
The scene changed in her eyes
I knew it was the second truth
That was whispering itself in a soft voice,

I leaned closer
Saw a glimpse of nature smiling
Even though everything is hurting her
She is just surviving

I saw her smile
Changing to Ruth,
And there it was
The third and the last painful truth,

It was me in her eyes
I saw my very own reflection,
For the time
I didn't pray for its perfection,

It was the real me filled with flaws
Not trying to hide in disguise,
I loved myself pure,
There in her eyes,

She blinked
Then looked at me
It was like we talked for eternity
The truth was all I could see

Again she unfolded her wings
Flew above retracting her track
I looked at her
But she never looked back.

_WH

Streets Of Life

Walking down
The street of life
Not knowing where it leads
Just following a quiet tune,

Stumbling upon the stones of emotions
Scattered here and there
The joy, the fear, the love or
The pain we share,

Thought I came to the end but
There came the whisper of my heart
He said, “It’s just the beginning
The mystery still lies beneath the art,”

Gathering the pieces of the puzzle
I started walling again
Walking down the street of mystery
As life demands.

_ WH

Semicolon

Maybe I'm a 'perhaps' in someone else's story
That they couldn't amend
Doesn't matter
I'm a semicolon in mine
A coma afraid to continue
With a full stop that refused to end.

But sometimes
Just sometimes I don't want to be a maybe
But rather a 'definitely'
I want that full stop removed
And that coma to continue freely,

However,
It's all just a 'maybe someday'
A story that hasn't ended
But paused as they say,

Like a text in drafts,
They couldn't send,
Maybe I'll always be a 'semicolon'
That couldn't end.

_WH

I Love My 3 Ams

I love my 3 ams
A three am painting sessions
When the kid in me becomes an artist
Painting little confessions

A three am writer
Maybe even worse, a poet
That whispers the screaming words
In the quiet,

A three am therapist
Giving motivation, or perhaps
Telling that life doesn't end
With a cut on the wrist,

A three am philosopher
Writing philosophies
For unexpected love, we fell for,

A three am listener
Who Listens to the silence of the world
Changing slowly sometimes faster,

A three am speaker,
Who speaks only in front of her
A three am singer,
Singing mismatched melodies
While dancing like a lost drinker

Yes It’s only three ams
When life feels like a rollercoaster
Not like stupid trams.
That's why I love my 3 ams

_WH

Manuscripts

I still re-read the manuscripts
I wrote a decade ago,
Why?
I don't know,

Those poems stories
All the unsent letters
Somehow gave my heart warmth
you feel in an old worn out sweater,

Those words written
with an ink-dipped pen
Urges me to read them
Again and again,

Who thought
That old brown paper could feel like home,
A strange place that is unknown
But still somehow known,

I still reread the manuscripts
I wrote a decade ago,
Probably to find the real me
that I couldn't show.

_WH

Sad

Sad
The word whose real meaning is almost forgotten
A feeling that everyone wants to abandon,
What is sad?
Or what is like being sad?
When the raindrop falls
from heavy cloud
When the tear slips off your cheek
Silently instead of being loud
That is when you know
The condition of your heart is bad
That is when you feel
The real sad,
It is not sad when your heart breaks
It is not sad when you have to smile fake,
It is surely not sad when you cry for your sake
It is sad when your heart is shattered and destroyed
It is sad when you have to smile to fill that one big void,
It is sad when you want to cry but the tears ain't comin,
It is sad when you choose to stay instead of runnin,
A three letter word holding the weight of our emotions
Like a stone attached to a line
You know you are sad when someone asks how are you and
All you say is "I AM FINE."

_WH

Flower Shop

I passed a flower shop today,
The same one that always convinces me to stay
Just not this time,
Not anymore,
The picture of the same old white rose clouded my mind,
With that picture, came a Memory,
The one that I tried to bury
In my heart's cemetery,
But I still remember
The night when someone asked you about my favorite flower,
Without missing a beat you said
She doesn't have any, nothing suits her,
Hiding the pain I smiled happily instead,
But something died that night
The roses in my vase couldn't gleam white,
I couldn't stop at the flower shop ever since,
Just like today,
No matter how hard the petals convince.

_WH

Dead Roses

They say,
Fresh roses contain love and fragrance,
But I say
The dead ones contain memories of once alive romance
The ones that died in the wait
Of unrequited love for someone,
Are the ones I still keep
With those letters, I couldn't burn,
The dead fragrance
Scenting the pages of my once favorite book,
With imprints on the manuscript,
I'm afraid to look,
The dried Petals
Falling on the cold land
Reminds me of you holding them
With a ring in another hand,
So yeah the red roses might contain love and fragrance
But my dear,
The Dead Roses contains me
And your presence.

_WH

I Wonder

I wonder how much pain a writer
Must have hidden under the line,
I wonder how loved a poet
Must have felt that his voice couldn't defined,
I wonder how joyful the person
Must have felt when he wrote the nursery rhyme,
I wonder how happy the child
Must have felt when he first colored his very own design,
I wonder how magical the astronomer
Must have felt when he first noticed the stars that align,
I wonder how energetic the person
Must have felt when he drank the coffee for the first time,
I wonder how proud an actor
Must have felt when his name, written was no longer just a sign,
I wonder and wonder
How our small heart keeps all of these emotions and feelings enshrined.

_WH

Did They?

Did they even notice?
The scars I hid
Under my long sleeves
I wanted to confess
But a part of me said "They'll never believe,"

My feelings were buried
In the grave of my own head
I was shouting
I was screaming
Crying to be dead,

I wanted freedom
Not from the world
But from my own self
I cried to help me
But they all listened
Like deaf,

Did they ever found?
The traces of broken me
I tried to fix all night
Or the part of real me I hid
Under the broad daylight,

Did they ever saw?
My suffering soul
In the cage of my mind
Even if they noticed
Then why did they turn blind?

Did they ever hear?
My silent tears
Falling without making any sound
Or my silent pleas, I cried
When the pool of my thoughts made me drown,

Did they ever wonder?
From where I got those burning patches
Craved beautifully on my thighs
Or did they believe the lie
That I was okay, to all their whys,

But now I think there's no point
In asking these questions to them
Cause they never cared
Listened
Or felt my pain,

The pain of rotting
Inside the shell of your own body
The pain of not being understood
By somebody,

The pain that no one can see
Which kills me from within
The pain of burning
I felt on my cold skin,

The pain I could feel
Holding the knife
The pain that will disappear
When I stop my breath
And end my life.

_WH

Nine Seconds

Standing in the middle of the hallway
Classrooms across each other, close yet so far away
Like 31 December and 1st Jan, we have been
Always separated by a day of yes or no in between,
Looking into his eyes
In hope to find my answer
The eight seconds of courage broke
Like a glass shatter
He doesn't feel it too
It's just stupid me
He doesn't love me too
It's just the delusions I see
All these doubts I started feeling on my skin
My heart raced back from the illusionistic astray
Taking the ninth second in
Like always I looked away"

_WH

In A World

In a world full of deaf listeners
An artist sings the song of his heart
In the hope that someday
Someone will embrace his art,

In a world full of trendy liars,
An old painting is still waiting
For its silent admirer,

In the world full of blind critics
A poem is somewhere
Afraid to express its lyrics,

In a world full of fake feelings
Misjudging a story
A writer is trying to hide
His untold glory,

In a world full of people
Who are just alive
We my love live
Are trying to survive.

_WH

He Looked At Me!

He looked at me
Like there was something in me worth looking at.
After such a long time I felt
I meant something to someone like a girl with an aching heart.
Longing for someone's love,
someone's touch to make me realise that I was alive,
When he looked at me
I found the traces of my feelings
I buried in an archive,
Hidden from everyone
So that no one can see
But he saw
And now I'm afraid
I'm afraid I'm falling for him in a one-sided love
Which l like to call one-sided trade
I'm afraid I've started loving him
But he will never love me back
And when his crushing era will end,
My heart will again be left with an incurable crack
Despite all of this
I still want to give it a try
Because I saw a piece of me
In the look of his eye.

_WH

Holding Onto Ifs And Buts

I can go months pretending
I forgot about you
But deep down it's only you
I think about in the days and nights too
If I ever sit down
Think about all the wishes I asked for fun
You'll always be my favourite
But an incomplete one,
Sometimes I wonder what I liked about you
What made me fall so hard?
Maybe your brown hair
The smile on your lips
The blush on your cheeks that blossom
When you laugh
Or maybe it was the look of your honey eyes
That I still adore,
Sometimes I wonder what it would be like to be loved by you,
Guess now I couldn't find the answer
Cause you never loved me too,
Sometimes I wish I never met you
Maybe things would have been different
And my world wouldn't have turned blue
Sometimes I wish I never sent you that text
May be our us in my mind would have been different
And my heart wouldn't be wrecked,
Now it's over, the feeling of us
But I can't move on
As I'm still holding on to ifs and buts.

_WH

Living With The Heart Is A Tragedy

Don't ask me where my heart lives
I'm afraid I won't answer the world you belong to,
I'm also afraid as the answer is still unknown to me to be true,
But I wonder
I wonder if it is left somewhere between the pages of the book
I once read,
Or is it in the bunch of roses in the vase
Waiting to be dead,
I wonder if it is still inside of me
Or does it stay behind in the moments
I spent with you under that old oaktree,
It's maybe lost somewhere
But I'm still living happily
Maybe Cause sometimes I think
Living with the heart was also a tragedy.

_WH

Anyway

I knew how it was gonna end
But I still loved you,
Anyway,
I know I wouldn't be able to let you go
But I said goodbye
Anyway,
Yes I wanted to pretend I was strong
But I let my tears fall
Anyway,
I know I should forget you now
But I still want to hold on to everything
Anyway,
I know my phone's screen will not brighten up with your messages
But I'm still staring at it
Anyway,
My story was something who's ending I knew
But I watched it again,
Anyway,
I knew you were never mine
But I still loved you,
Anyway.

_WH

Not Every Sorry Deserves An "It's Okay" In Return

Not every sorry deserves an "It's Okay"
In return
This is the notion of this selfish era
You should now learn

You say sorry to heal what's hurt
Like a broken heart with a deep crack
Or the words you can't take back,

But they say sorry to play with your feelings
And hurt you even when they know
You are still healing,

Not every sorry deserves and "it's alright"
In reply
Cause people just say sorry
For their bad deeds to justify,

Don't fell in the trap
Of their hopeful manipulative words,
There is more than this
Your heart deserves,

Not every sorry deserves and "it's fine"
In reply
Your heart knows
Those words
Are just another bunch of lies.

_WH

Jake Didn't Fall For Rose

Hiding behind the door
Of his room
Listening to him talking about me
With his friend in a soft tune

"Why her, Jake?" His friend asked,
"It's just her everywhere"
He answered without missing a beat
I could feel my breath gasped,
I kept quiet listening to his words about me
He said," just her everywhere I see"

"Her eyes are what I want to see every morning
I wake,
Her words are what I want to hear,
Her hair is what I want to touch and her smile,
oh her sweet smile makes me go crazy
for god's sake!

I think I'm in love with her
I'm going insane
Last night I saw her dancing
softly in the rain,
I wanted to hold her
In my hands
I wanted to brush her wet hair strands,
And you ask me why my mind is always hers?
I don't know but I secretly loved her
All these stupid years!"

I could feel tears
Threatening to fall down my cheeks
While listening to him
Cause I know it wasn't me,
I was never mentioned in his hymn,
I saw him watching her,
With pain in my heart
Water dripping from my clothes,
Because this time
Jake didn't fall for Rose.

_WH

You and I, our Us Is Beautiful

It's beautiful
You and I
Our us is beautiful
The feeling,
Of Your thoughts lingering in my mind,
Is beautiful,
The way your name brings a smile to my lips
Is beautiful,
My eyes searching for you
Is beautiful,
Your looking back when I'm staring at you
Is beautiful,
My calling and your staying
Is beautiful,
My talking and your listening
Is beautiful,
But then you ask what's beautiful
And I say
You and I
The us in my mind
is beautiful.

_WH

A Thousand Miles Apart

We're a thousand miles apart
Maybe more,
But I still feel your heart
Sitting beside a seashore,

You know I hate you for breaking the promise
to be with me forever
but I can forgive you because of the moments
we spend together,

Yes I know I promise to follow your soul
from this world to the very end
but there's a writing of the fate
I still couldn't amend

wished you were here
sitting beside me
but the world without you
is all I could see,

now I am here sitting
beside your grave
with all my strength
pretending to be brave,

my heart is mourning
but the water is scared to fall from my eye,
because of the promise I made
that I will not cry,

We're a thousand miles apart
Maybe more
but I still feel your heart
Cause' there's nothing left
to feel any more.

_WH

The Last Memory

It should be suffocating
I should be gasping for air
But all I felt was serene
All I herald was silent prayers,

My heart has now stopped hurting
I wonder
Why it wasn't beating

The stroms inside me
Went away with the waves
I realised they were finally going to lay me
Six feet under with other graves,

I wonder
Why my loved ones couldn't hear my cries
I fealt each of the tear they shed
Everything started making sense
When I saw myself dressed up
In a decorated bed,

People were reciting eulogies
But somewhere the silence was killing
Filled with sorrow my heart felt relieved
Even though they were sad
Still my family was smiling,

A smile was too on my face
But tears rolled down from my eyes
As the angel of death held my hand
Pointed where the end door lies,

Tears flowed down
As I asked for few moments more
But silently she nodded her head
Whipping off my tears
I walked few feets towards the end shore.

_WH

I Met A Stranger Who Knew My Name

I saw you today
Yes, I saw you today
At least that's what my heart says,
It's been four months and 7 days
But who's counting anyway?
It almost felt the same as when we first met
I couldn't remember the weather
We were busy talking till sunset
Maybe today when I saw you
The weather was still the same
But something seemed different
This time
I met a stranger who knew my name
This time I met a stranger who somehow is there
In my memory
A stranger who knows my favourite flower
Is a rose, of colour ivory,
A stranger who knew everything
whether it's my favourite food, colour or even my favourite book,
A stranger who once couldn't survive a day without seeing me
Just passed by me and not even trying to look,
I was at the same place where one stranger promised that he will stay
The same place where I saw you
Yes I saw you today
At least that's what I think my heart says.

_WH

How Fast We Grew Up

Stories have already been written
But secretly we wish on falling stars,
For something that maybe god forgot
To mention in the fate of ours.
Wishing every night for our lives
To change all of sudden,
At the same time claiming the magic and pixie dust
To be just a childhood burden.
"I'm grown up now! I don't watch cartoons" the adults lie.
The same ones whose eyes still filled with tears
When they saw piko watching Riruru almost die,
Sometimes I find it funny to think
we were the kids who laughed and snot,
We used to play in the empty streets and
One day decided we should not,
"Something is changed" we say,
Yes, we are grown up now
But that does not means the child in us couldn't stay.

_WH

Bruised Angel With A Broken Wing

Life isn't a fairytale anymore
It doesn't feel magical
Like it felt before,
Now no more waiting for a kneeled prince
Holding a ring
All that is left is a bruised angel
With a broken wing
The wings that fluttered
Torned and ripped off by her own people
That lit a fire in her
Now I'm afraid
Her revenge will be lethal,
The angels on her shoulders were cast off
The tiara that once represented her kindness
Was burned off,
The long lost broken princess
Was all gone
Now the devil has taken the throne,
With venom in her tone
Evilness she never shown
She became the most ruthless queen
Ever known,
She never actually existed in real
She is a feeling in all of us
Who are broken and couldn't heal,
She is someone showing you a path
To turn your brokenness
Into your wrath
Now is the time to understand that
A broken glass does more damage
Then the one who is smooth and flat.

_WH

A Home

The place where at the end of the day
Someone will still be waiting for you
A place you can always turn to,
Even when everyone turns their back on you
There will be a place
Where people only love you,
The place that gave you sweet and sour memories
The place where you can eat without thinking of calories
The place that lives inside you
Like a sweet fragrance of rosemaries,
The only place in the world
Where you are more than just comfortable
It is the only place
Where you don't have to always pretend impressible,
Ever wonder how a four-letter word
Can bring a huge smile to our face
It's like a series of emotion
No one can replace,
The place where at the end of the day
Someone will still be waiting for us
A home we all blindly trust.

_WH

I Want To Learn How To Unlove Him

I don't know if unlove is even a word or not
But I still want to learn how to unlove him
Because I can't
My heart still sings his memories
Like an unforgotten hymn
He is so embedded in me
I just can't get him out of my mind,
I don't know how to untangle the string of my thoughts
That are so deeply intertwined,
I still remember the day I first saw him,
Fell into your eyes but looked away
It wasn't love at first sight,
Rather it grew slowly and
Quietly every moment every day,
Minute after minute,
Day after day
Month after month passed
I still say I didn't count the time,
I just got soo invested in someone
Who wasn't even mine,
You said my confession was unexpected but I knew your answer
Yet I still give it a try,
However I never expected,
For my eyes to cry,
I cried and cried every night begging God to remove his memories,
his smile from my soul and my heart
My prayers went in vain
I watched myself falling apart
And I couldn't do anything
I never wanted to see him again
Wished he never comes back in my life

But a part of me still ached for him
Like I've been stabbed by a knife,
Like multiple time Right here in my heart
The wounds are not visible
But it still pains a lot,
I don't know if unlove is even a word or not
But I want to learn how to unlove him
Because I can't
He became someone I hate
At the same moment someone I want.

_WH

Our Wrong Timings

You know it still hurts
Sometimes I wonder
Why it didn't worked,
Maybe
We were not meant to be together
But
What was it with your promises
To be with me forever,
Maybe
For you every night I cried
Maybe
For us, you really tried
You said you'll always find your way
Back to me
But there was a straight path
You couldn't see,
You used to say
You can read me like an open book
But there was something
I wished you understood
Maybe
The universe gave us signs
You and I were perfect
But
We just met at the wrong time,
You know it still hurts
Sometimes I think
Living with you was worse.

_WH

Just A Silly Crush

Every time I sat down
To write you a poem
Don't know why but my lines
couldn't catch its rhythm,

All these years
I have been sharing my feelings through my words,
But when it comes to you
I don't know why my vocab couldn't find the letter you deserve,

After a long thought
I finally found some,
Just read it, cause talking to you
kind of makes my heart feel numb,

Whenever I put a story one or two
Sometimes just sometimes
It's directed to you,
I tried really hard to ignore you
whenever you were around
Cause little did you know it's your eyes
That made me want to drown,

Minutes after minutes
My eyes searched the room for you
Deep down wishing
You see me too,

I don't think you remember sending hearts
To my poem one day,
But that simple gesture is something
I still can't forget anyway,
I wanted to confess but a part of me believed
You didn't think of me more than a classmate
Call me hopeful but I still think
Meeting you was somewhere written in our fate,

All I wished a little time with you
Or a few talks more
To say a couple of words
I couldn't say before,
But now it feels
The words are better left unsaid,
We both have a separate paths ahead.

_WH

Look At Me

Look at me
Didn't my eyes tell you?
You are one
They found wherever they see
Or didn't my smile express it to you
When you're around then only it feels free,
Didn't my cheeks tell you?
That they only blossom at the words
You randomly say
Didn't my lips express it to you?
That you are the one they ever begged
For a little more to stay,
Or its just me thinking
You'll read my feelings in between the lines
While you are the only one
Ignoring my stupid signs.

_WH

Thinking You'll Come Back To Me

Thinking you'll come back to me
Is the same as
Thinking I could touch the sky
Standing on an average height
Or thinking I could find stars
On a dark cloudy night,
Wishing you'll love me again
Is the same as
Wishing on a shooting star
Which is too falling
Or wishing on a copper coin
Which is too drowning
I'm tired of this
Thinking and wishing
I'm tired of the thought that you went
And something inside me is still missing,
You never cared about me
When we were together
Now I'm tired but some pieces of my heart
Are still left for me to gather.

_WH

Night Time

The time of the day
Most people fear
The time of the day
When I am free
To shed my tear,

The time of the day
When everything is counsumed by darkness
The time of the day
When I sofeten my cover of hardness,

When most of the voice
Of the world are silenced
The soft screams of my thoughts
Are intensed,

The time when
People are busy creating their fantasy
Is the same time
I use to escape my reality,

The time looking at the sky
Noticing stars chanding their positisions
As if telling me
Never stop chasing my ambitions,

The time of the day
When rooms are filled with snoring sounds
The same time
When i let the train of my thoughts
Circle around,

The time of the day
Most people fear
But it is the only time
When I used to think like shakespear.

_WH

Life Is A Journey

Let the moments freeze
Just feel the cold and warm breeze,

Don't always run blindly
In those endless races
Take a pause
Think about life's
Different phases,

Take a minute
Appreciate yourself for coming
All the way here
Whether going through sweet memories
Or dodging off your fear,

I know life isn't sweet
Like a piece of cake
But it can be tasty
Like a tangy lemonade,

Enjoy every sip of it
Just live a little
Rather than exit,

Stop trying to fit
In the format
There is alot more
Out of our natural habitat,

Fall in love
Fall apart
Never be afraid
To make a new start

Remember
Life isn't a marry go round
Its a journey
That goes left, right
Up and down.

_WH

Diffrent Me For Every You

My whole life I spent pretending
Something I was not
Different, me for every, you
A different person to you,
A different person to them.
But now I realised
That while dodging between those multiple personality
I lost the real me
Maybe somewhere in the middle
Or maybe I lost it when I tried
To become something I was not,
Different, me for every, you
We all have heard that everyone needs someone special
So while becoming everyones special One
I forgot I was also included in that everyone,
And now I'm just someone,
Now I have become just something I was not
Different me for every you.

_WH

The Time I Paused

It's a bitter truth
No matter how much u try the things don't go back like it was before
A sweet lie
Like the ocean in a bottle will always find a shore,
Or
The god above listen and gives u what u prayed for
But no
Begging and crying for that one had made my eyes sore,
Tried of floating
Tired of surviving
I gave up on every hope of reviving
Now I watch as I slowly sank down
Slowly I watched myself drown
Under the water of grief
I found pieces of relief
I know I couldn't make things as it was
But I'll find you and me in the time I paused.

_WH

What Is Love?

When I look at you
I think you were my fated muse,
but when I try to paint your portrait with the bright colours
My Canvas turned dark with the ones I never used,
That's when I wonder,
Is love something to be afraid of?
Or its just some other emotions
We named love
Then what is love?
I started to think
Is it somewhere described
In a poet's ink?
A poem written for his lover
Words drenched in feelings
Is that his love he had for her?
Is it love if my heart raced
when our eyes collide?
Or the emotion I felt
When I saw you with someone and my eyes cried,
If that is love to you
Then should I be afraid
Cause I know you'll never love me too.

_WH

Coffin Of Memories

We never forget Bad memories
They just hide in the darkest corner of our mind
Slowly slowly our mind becomes a coffin of memories
buried in the graveyard
We named "past".

-WH

Acknowledgment

This little book of poems is a piece of my heart, but it wouldn't have been possible without the love and magic of the people around me.
This book is a patchwork quilt of memories, love, and dreams, stitched together with the kindness and encouragement of so many wonderful souls. As I write this acknowledgment, I'm filled with immense gratitude for the people and moments that made this journey possible.

To my family, for always being my biggest cheerleaders and believing in my dreams (even the wild ones). You've taught me that dreams are worth chasing and that love is the greatest gift of all.
Mom and Dad, thank you for believing in my dreams, even when they seemed like whispers in the wind. Your constant encouragement gave me the strength to put my heart into these pages. your belief in me has been the anchor in every storm.
Thank you for the love that has been the sun in my dark life who always helped me bloom.

To my friends, who have always been there whenever I needed them. You've reminded me that life is a tapestry woven with love and connection. Your enthusiasm for my work has kept me going even on the toughest days, whether it's two in the morning or late evening, you have listened to and reviewed these poems for me.
Without your contribution, this book would never been here.
Thank you for being my sounding board, cheering me on, and celebrating every small victory with me.

To the countless cups of coffee and cozy blankets, thank you for being the quiet companions during late-night scribbles.
To the books that have
helped me create my own world of fiction and live through the world of harsh reality. Thank you for making me a proud reader

To the little moments of life, the morning sun streaming through the curtains, the sound of rain on a quiet evening, the little twinkling of stars at night, and the soft brushes of winds on my skin every time I felt alone.
Thank you for inspiring me to find beauty in the every day and joy in living reality.

To the quiet, unassuming moments of solitude that allowed me to dream, to write, and to reflect.
Thank you for reminding me that creativity often blooms in stillness. It's in those quiet hours, with a cozy blanket wrapped around me, that I've found not only my words but also myself.

Lastly to my readers

Dear reader,

Thank you for opening this book and stepping into the world of my words.

From the moment this collection began to take shape, I imagined someone like you holding it in their hands. Whether you're reading in the soft glow of morning sunlight, curled up under a blanket on a rainy afternoon, or stealing quiet moments in the middle of a busy day

I am so grateful that my words are accompanying you, even for a little while.Thank you for being you for bringing your unique perspective, your open heart, and your beautiful mind to these poems.

Thank you for taking the time to step into this world with me. And most of all, thank you for reminding me why stories and emotions matter so much: because they bring us closer together.

Each poem here is like a love letter to life, and I hope you find pieces of your own story tucked into these verses.

Knowing my words might touch your heart fills me with immeasurable joy.

With all my love and gratitude,

White Hunter

About The Author

White Hunter has always been someone who found magic in the little things. From a young age, they were captivated by the beauty of the world around them—watching birds flutter outside their window, collecting shiny pebbles during walks, and crafting tiny stories about the woodland creatures they imagined lived just out of sight.

As a child, she spent countless afternoons with a notebook in hand, scribbling down observations and creating whimsical tales inspired by their surroundings. Their love for words and storytelling blossomed under the gentle encouragement of family and teachers, who always reminded them that even the quietest voices have the power to be heard.

Her path to becoming a writer wasn't straightforward, but it was filled with heartwarming twists and turns. They tried their hand at many things, painting crocheting, maths, and science before finally realizing that their true calling lay in putting pen to paper. Their ability to find joy and meaning in life's everyday moments became the foundation of their writing style, which is often described as a warm hug in literary form.

Outside of their writing, White Hunter is a self-proclaimed lover of all things cozy. Their perfect day starts with a freezing cup of cold coffee, a fuzzy pair of socks, and the company of their beloved books. They adore rainy afternoons spent curled up by the window, where the sound of droplets tapping on the glass fuels their creativity.

Nature plays a special role in her life, and much of their inspiration comes from the simple pleasures of reading books and writing stories and poems. They often say that the world has a funny way of sharing its stories, whether it's through the chirp of a cricket or the smell of rain on a summer evening. All you have to do is listen.

In addition to writing, White Hunter loves connecting with readers and hearing how their stories resonate with others. They believe that words have a unique power to bring people together, to remind us that even though we may lead different lives, we all share a deep yearning for love, comfort, and a sense of belonging. Their little corner of the world is filled with bookshelves that stretch to the ceiling, cozy blankets draped over every chair, and the scent of freshly baked cookies wafting from the kitchen. It's the kind of place where stories come alive and laughter feels like music.

Through their work, White Hunter hopes to remind readers that life's most precious moments are often found in the quiet, unassuming corners of our days. Their writing is a heartfelt celebration of the warmth, wonder, and whimsy that make life beautiful.

This book is a reflection of the journey they've taken—a collection of lessons, love, and the quiet magic that's been woven into their world. It is their sincerest hope that these pages bring a smile to your face, a little extra light to your day, and a gentle reminder that joy can always be found if you know where to look.

THANK YOU FOR READING

www.ingramcontent.com/pod-product-compliance
Lightning Source LLC
LaVergne TN
LVHW041230150826
845673LV00008B/2343

* 9 7 9 8 8 9 6 3 2 9 3 9 8 *